SEX

Before Marriage.
What's the harm?

(C) 2008 Daniele Luciano Moskal

ISBN 0-9545113-4-4
Unique Writing Publications (UK)

Unless otherwise indicated, all Scripture quotations are taken from the *King James Version* (KJV), of the Holy Bible.

Unique
WRITING PUBLICATIONS

CONTENTS

FOREWORD

SEX *n.* state of being male or female; males or females

collectively; sexual intercourse - act of procreation in which male's

penis is inserted into female's vagina

(Collins Gem English Dictionary)
© Wm. Collins Sons & Co. Ltd
1902, 1936, 1954, 1963, 1981.

DEDICATION

I dedicate this book to all the young and old people of this world

who have struggled with this one particular question at one point

of their lives. May your eyes be truly opened through this book

to the everlasting truth of God's Holy Word concerning

"Sex before Marriage, what's the harm?"

From the Author

Making moral judgements in today's society is far from easy. The complexities of modern life in this world today can make moral decision-making about as intricate a business as picking a route through the crowded streets of a large city. Add the fact that many of these decisions have to be taken on the spur of the moment, and clear moral sign-posts become essential. So where are we to find them?

The answer that springs most easily to the Christian's mind is *'in the Holy Bible.'* The Holy Bible is God's Word. As Christians, we believe that God still speaks to us through its pages. It is to God's Holy Word, therefore, that we turn first for guidance in the moral problems we meet. The Holy Bible is God's own demister. It answers the most basic questions anyone can ask about morality: *"What is good?"* and *"What is right?"*

As Christians we need the Word of God as a ship's captain needs his radar in a sea fog. Every contemporary moral issue raises fundamental questions of right and wrong which sometimes lurk just below the surface, and in any moral dilemma, making the right decision is only stage one.

Stage two - carrying the decision into practice - is much harder. For example, we do not need anyone to tell us that generosity is right and bad-temperedness wrong; but in practice we know we are sometimes stingy and occasionally lose our temper. In other words, we lack the will-power to carry through the decisions we make quite sensibly in our minds. At this level the Holy Bible offers us a unique source of help. Some books on morality will convince us that we ought to live better lives. A few may even inspire us to make greater efforts. But in pointing us to the almighty God the Scriptures do far more than that. They direct us to a source of moral power which can overcome our weakness and make us free to do the right thing as well as avoid the wrong. Some people caricature the Holy Bible as a book which is full of *"Thou shalt not's."* That is unfair. In fact, its central message is a triumphant 'You *can* - in God's power' (Philippians 4:13).

So the Holy Bible is more than a guide book. It is God's power tool. It stimulates us to work out moral judgements that are really sound - because they are based on mainline principles. It also serves as a unique contemporary teaching book simply because it directs us to those tough everyday moral questions like *"What's the harm in sex before marriage?"*, and gives us God's mind on them. In researching and asking teenagers many questions concerning this subject over a couple of years and eventually writing this challenging book, my prayer is that you will believe me when I say that there is no more cogent argument to drive us back to the Holy Bible as our uniquely relevant, adequate and necessary guide in living the moral life here on earth, as God intended. God Bless you as you read on…..

- JOHN 3:34 Evangelist Daniele Luciano Moskal

LOVE & SEX

Falling head-over-heels in *Love* is for many an unforgettable experience. One day life seems to be going on in much the usual way and the next - WHAM BAM! You soon discover that real love isn't just chocolates and roses, and lovey-dovey notes left underneath pillows or on fridge doors, or carving your sweet-heart's name on the trunk of a tree, or sending a valentine's card or text message – it's much more than that!!

Many of the world's best Poets and songwriters of today's modern world have tried to capture the champagne feeling but, honestly, can you really put it in words? Yes, but then there's the Sex thing to consider as well. It's marvellous when it goes right but hell when it doesn't. I believe it was Tolstoy who once said: *"That the world's greatest tragedy was the bedroom"*. Put the two together - Sex and falling in love - and you've got the most explosive potential known to man (feminists please add 'and woman').

Christians, being human, are no different from anybody else when it comes to the experiences of sex and falling in love. So, we Christians also feel our sexuality and its potency just as much as anyone else and we'd be in a much worse state if we didn't. There's nothing wrong about feeling the power of erotic love and its physical and emotional aspects. Isn't it strange that I, a Pastor, a Minister of the "Gospel" need to have to say that? Strange, that a Christian has to defend sexuality as a God-given thing? But, you open your Holy Bible and you come to the Song of Songs, the Song of Solomon. There it is, an oriental love poem extolling the beauty of the beloved and the desirability of making love to such a wonderful person. It's there in God's Holy Bible. Lush imagery, warm with passion, taught with unfulfilled desire. So why is it found in the Holy Bible? For one reason to show that God who created human beings in His own image, and planned that *'the two shall become one flesh'* (Genesis chapter 2 verse 23-25), meant it to be that way.

Adam the first man joyfully recognised that he and Eve belonged together. As verse 24 suggests, this suitability is the basis for all marriages. This passage was also quoted by Jesus the founder of Christianity, in the book of (Matthew 19:5; and Mark 10:7-8), and by Apostle Paul (1 Corinthians 6:16; Ephesians 5:31), in their comments on sex and marriage. How sad it is that Christians down the ages have warped it and twisted it until some of them have become ashamed even to think of their own or another's sexuality.

Sex (in the sense of sexuality), is good, glorious and God-inspired. It's not a dirty word, because God is not a dirty God. He's a Holy righteous God, who loves holiness and hates sin. Sex is a part of my humanity, a great creative aspect of my *being-made-in-His-image* and I will as a Christian not debase it into a sordid, shameful, guilt-ridden desire, to be kept under and repressed. But this world unfortunately is not short of fools. And the foolish ones have managed to get things upside down. And the foolish ones have really made a fine old mess when it comes to Sex.

"The fool has said to himself: There is no God".

(Psalm 14:1).

In today's twentieth-century modern Great Britain, there are plenty of fools like that whose lives admit of no God, no creator, no master, and so, quite logically, of no restraints upon their behaviour. For them, sex is an appetite to be satisfied as and when they wish and with whom they wish. No Christian can possibly accept their view of life or their way of living it.

As Christians we have pledged allegiance to our God - it is as simple statement we make to Him for our lives:

"I am a man/woman under authority. I am not my own master. I have been bought and redeemed for an unbelievable price - the life-blood of Jesus Christ of Nazareth, the Son of the true and living God!"

SO, ZIP IT UP!

Yes, my friend, yes my brother, yes my sister. That means just this. Jesus Christ, said the Law (God's Holy Word), was not a set of regulations to be studied for loopholes, but it was the voice of God talking about practical truth and love. In Jesus' speech on the Sermon on the Mount (see Matthew 5:27-32), before He mentioned divorce He spoke of adultery, and in both cases He made us look at the realities of our behaviour, not the legal niceties - for we may be comfortable within the law in our acts and right outside in our thoughts; or unassailable on our rights and damnable in our relationships.

But in the Gospel of Matthew chapter 19, Jesus Christ went further still. He pointed out that marriage involves you with your Creator, and it is His work you pull apart when you get a divorce or commit adultery or fornication, or have sex outside marriage. Jesus Christ put it unforgettable words, in a phrase the whole marriage service world-wide has borrowed for its moment of climax, (usually before the bride and groom have been asked by the host to kiss one another): *"What …. God has joined together, let no man put asunder"* (Matthew 19:6).

The Genesis creation story shows what Marriage truly is; the divorce law shows only what mankind has become.

Marriage is a covenant relationship, and God's Word says, *"Marriage is honourable in all, and the bed undefiled."* (Hebrews 13:4).

So Sex is the sign of a covenant relationship between a man and a woman. The covenant is why God gave Sex only to those who are married. Sex wasn't made for lusting and getting, it was made for loving and giving. Love gives, lust gets. Lust is perverted love. Sex is sacred to a marriage, because Sex is for marriage. Sex was given as an act of God's love, not lust. Lust is never satisfied; love is easily satisfied. Sex is not something to be ashamed of, avoided, denied or secretly lusted after. It is something lovely, good, holy, decent and most importantly in keeping with the covenant relationship between a man and woman. Love is satisfying, lust is insatiable, and love cannot exist without relationship. It can only be manifested when there is an object to be loved.

Relationship is personal, and so is salvation. All that we ever need, desire or want in life can be found in the Lord Jesus Christ and He always satisfies fully. For God's Love is strong, trusting love, and love and trust walk hand in hand. For **God is LOVE, and nothing is stronger than LOVE, and nothing is stronger than God's LOVE!**

Christianity is the only religion that has elevated a woman to the place God originally created her to be - that of joint-heir with man, a *'Help Meet'*, in Marriage. ***"For this cause shall a man leave his father and mother, and shall be joined unto his wife, and they two shall be one flesh. This is a great mystery: but I speak*** *concerning Christ and the church."* (Ephesians 5: 31-32).

God is the author, developer and finisher of marriage. For God said it was not good for man to be alone. How right He was. How gracious to make that woman. In marriage a man and woman rightly retain the ring. The wedding ring worn is always gold, because it is the most precious and valuable of all metals. What is more valuable than marriage, I ask you? The wedding ring also has no end, neither should marriage!

Men often complain that they do not understand women, but often they simply do not understand themselves. A woman's uniqueness is her greatest appeal to a man - and his greatest challenge. A woman was made to be beautiful, desirable and loved, and she glories in her relationship to a man in love and marriage because he manifests the nature and image of Christ-likeness. Woman was not taken from man's head to rule. She was not taken from his feet to be trampled upon like a doormat. NO! She was taken from near his heart to be loved and from under his arm to be protected.

From the very beginning in the Garden of Eden, the Genesis story you will notice that marriage was instituted in the time of man's innocence. Its first law was crystal clear. It is the top human relationship and all others, no matter how close, must be forsaken for it. Marriage should be an anchorage for both parties, the place of rest in one another's love and companionship.

In marriage the Holy Bible teaches the man and wife are heirs of the grace of life. Marriage is about giving, not taking. When a man and woman fall in love and decide to marry, they must realise they are marrying everything they are and everything they've been in the past. So be patient! You may not see immediate change in your spouse. It takes time for even a small cut to heal. It's a process, and *so* is marriage. Ask God in prayer for His grace to minister to your spouse (and to the child within them). If you ask Him, God will give you the oil of compassion and the wine of love to pour into their wounds.

The Holy Bible teaches that we're not to be so super spiritual that we become non-existent, or unavailable. God says to the married couples of this world that we are to be concerned about pleasing our soul mates. He said that your first ministry is to your own home and your first calling is to your own spouse. Your priorities need to start there, and then they will spread to your career, your vocation and other pursuits. As a brother in Christ once spoke to me: ***"God builds the house, but we have to do our own decorating!"***

When a man and woman marry they become one body, one bone, one flesh of each other; that missing rib which was taken from man (Adam) has now been firmly placed back at his side (Eve). In Marriage, you also inherit your partner's strengths, their fears and their weaknesses. And it's impossible to choose the best parts you want and leave the bad ones you don't. God said it's a package deal!

As a married Christian I gladly accept that my sexuality is God-given. But I also sadly accept that my sexuality is a field ripe for self-exploitation. It's one aspect of my sinful nature. Only one, but it's still there and I dare not delude myself into forgetting it. It's not my sexuality that's shameful it's me!

So I treat Sex all and that goes with it with respect. I know it can be great as an experience. And I know too that it can go wrong as an experience. But right or wrong, enjoyable or frustrating, as an experience is only one side of it. The other is the right or wrong of the actual motives and actions in moral terms.

DOING THE RIGHT THING

For the whole Sex and falling-in-love bit needs both to be right - the experience and the morality. Christians therefore accept what they believe to be creative restraint upon their sexuality. They don't go to bed with people at the drop of a hat (nor should it be a skirt or trousers). They don't treat each other's bodies as amusement arcades or mere fun palaces. They know the right thing; they know the way that their chemistry works and the powerful instincts which a bit of the old *'slap-and-tickle'* arouses. They are cautious about rushing into a wild embrace simply because it's enjoyable.

In other words, Christians believe in marriage or, to use the language of the sociologists, in permanent pair-bonding. They see the union of two bodies sexually as the symbol of total commitment - *"the two become one flesh"*, to which they add *'under one master - GOD!* And they keep sexual intercourse within that relationship. If we can get this foundation principle clear, you're on the right road to sorting out the practical questions which face every young unmarried boy or girl. Lots of people are very prone to *"falling in love"*. But my emotions alone are no sure guide to what is a right course of action. My feelings can be like a yo-yo. Only a fool lets his/her emotions, feelings, and moods, become master of their actions. And I have previously mentioned only a fool say's there is no God (Psalm 14:1).

I want to make this point very strongly to you the reader, that Sex is not a dirty word because God's not dirty, nor is He perverted and Sex is not an evil word because God is not evil. Nothing, absolutely nothing that God ever created could be dirty. The desire for Sex was God's idea - not ours. He placed this part of our nature into us; He created those chemicals (hormones) that make the opposite sex appealing to us as men and women. God did not make a man to lie down with a man, or a woman to lie down with a woman. God forbid! The Holy Bible and the Holy Scriptures speak plainly and truthfully, that it was **Adam and Eve** - not Adam and Steve, or Mary or Martha!!

God doesn't make mistakes; He's a perfect God who created man and woman in His perfect likeness and image for procreation. God created man and woman so we would have families of our own. Without this desire there would be no marriage and no children and no love between a man and woman. So Sex is not a dirty thing after all; it's a wonderful God thing, no matter what you have heard or read about it. However, I must also tell you my friend that God intends us to control that desire for sexual intercourse. He has stated repeatedly in the Holy Bible, that we are to save our bodies for the person we will eventually marry. For God warns us that it is absolutely wrong, unholy, to satisfy our appetite for sex with a man or woman before we get married. God's commandment that we avoid sexual intercourse before Marriage was not given in order to keep us from having pleasure. It wasn't God's desire to take fun out of life. On the contrary, it was actually His love that caused Him to forbid premarital intercourse, because so many harmful consequences occur when you refuse to obey Him.

Syphilis, Gonorrhoea, Aids, and other venereal diseases are very widespread today. Our society is witnessing an epidemic of these diseases, and they have a damaging effect on the body if they go untreated. But there are other consequences for those who have pre-marital Sex. They run the risk of bringing unwanted babies into the world by this act. When that occurs, they face the responsibility of raising a human being - a little life - a baby with all its needs for love and discipline and the stability of a loving home, but they have no way to take care of him/her or meet his/her needs. That is tragic.

Pre-marital Sex is a sin, and a person cannot be friends with God if he/she is going to continue to sin deliberately and wilfully. Furthermore, nothing can be hidden from God, as you should know by now He sees everything that is sinful. Sin always has a destructive effect on a young person's life. But I believe the sin of premarital sex is especially damaging to the person who engages in it. He or she loses the innocence of youth, and sometimes becomes hard and cold as a person. It's also likely to affect his or her later marriage, because that special experience which should have been shared with just one person is not so special anymore. More than one person has had a sample of it.

So you see my friend, there are many obvious reasons why God has told us to control our sexual desires. What I'm saying is that God has commanded us not to have Sex before Marriage in order to spare us these many other effects of this sin.

GOD'S SEX RULES

In the Book of Leviticus chapter 15, found in the Old Testament, God spoke to the people through His servant Moses concerning rules on Sex. Some of these rules regarding Sex and bodily discharges mystify modern readers, but the Israelites took for granted that God had dominion over the most private aspects of their lives. The Holy Bible does not provide a detailed rationale for these regulations. Some relate to health and hygiene: following the rules would help the Israelites avoid the venereal diseases that plagued their neighbours. Also, pagan religions commonly employed temple prostitutes, and God clearly intended for the Israelites to keep worship and Sex separate. Also, in chapter 18 of the same book of Leviticus, God speaks about Unlawful Sexual Relations, particular Child sacrifice and Sex. This warning against child sacrifice (repeated and expanded in 20:1-5), seems out of place in the middle of a chapter on rules about Sex. Yet, for the Israelites, there was a connection. Their neighbours, who sacrificed their children as a part of their religion, also practised temple prostitution as a way of worship. To them, Sex was a way to get in touch with their gods. God's warnings against various Sexual practices begin and end with warnings to behave differently from these neighbours (please **read verses 3, and 24 of chapter 18**).

In the Book of Judges chapter 2 and verse 13, God warns us concerning Fertility Gods. Israel's neighbours worshipped Baal and Ashoreth, male and female gods of fertility. Followers practised ritual Sex at the shrines, believing that Sex with sacred prostitutes led to good crops and many children. Sometimes, too, worshippers sacrificed their children to the gods. The Israelites' attraction to these foreign religions continued for most of their history as a nation. But *prostitution has* a literal meaning also. The religions Israel pursued taught that human sexuality was tied to agricultural fertility. To encourage good crops, believers in these religions practised their human fertility. This meant organised prostitution, done as part of their worship experience.

NAKED AND UNASHAMED

In the Book of Solomon *"Song of Songs"* found in the Old Testament, we are introduced to a poem with speaks about an intoxicating LOVE, a poem about what LOVE the way it's meant to be.

Chapter 8 and verse 7 says: **"Many waters cannot quench love; rivers cannot wash it away."** (NIV)

Flick the radio on, switch to any station, and what are you likely to hear? Love songs. Songs of new love, songs of disappointed love, songs of grateful love, songs of crazy love. Times change, but throughout history the flow of love songs is a constant. Plenty of people are shocked to find an explicit love song in the Holy Bible - complete with erotic lyrics. But Song of Songs is exactly that.

It shows no embarrassment about lovers enjoying each other's bodies, and talking about it. Consequently, intermittent attempts have been made to rule Song of Songs out of the Holy Bible or to make it for "Adults Only." In 16th-century Spain, for instance, professor Fray Luis de Leon was dragged out of his classroom and imprisoned for four years. What was his crime? He translated Song of Songs into Spanish.

Most Bible scholars believe that the poem was intended to celebrate love between married couples. God values Love between a man and woman. That's why He placed this song in His Holy Bible. It may have been sung first at a wedding.

These lovers are naked and unashamed; they love to look at each other. They love to tell each other what they feel. They revel in the sensuous: the beauty of nature, the scent of perfumes and spices. They are openly erotic. Their intoxication with love sounds quite up-to-date, not so different from what you hear on the radio. Yet

Song of Songs conveys a very different atmosphere from most modern love songs. The explicit lyrics never become even slightly dirty or perverted. This love comes straight from the Garden of Eden, when both man and woman were naked and unashamed. It is tender, filled with delight, natural love. You sense no shame or guilt; you feel that God is with the two as they love. The lovers act as equals. Both woman and man take the initiative in praising each other. They don't flirt or play games: they say what they mean. Yet they show caution and dignity in their love. While at the peak of joy, the lovers repeatedly warn others not to stir up love prematurely **(please read 2:7; 3:5; 8:4).** They recognise the dangerously explosive side of love. *"For love is as strong as death, its jealousy unyielding as the grave. It burns like blazing fire, like a mighty flame" (8:6).*

Song of Songs may be a difficult book to follow for some readers because one part doesn't seem connected to the next. But if you think of it as a series of photographs of a couple in love - snapshots not necessarily in order. Put together in one photo-album, they show the profound feelings of newly married lovers.

Though Song of Songs is primarily about love on the human level, many Christians and Jews have read it as a book about God's eternal love for us - a Love so rich, so full, and so unashamed. *(Now go and read the whole book for yourself)!*

SEXUAL SEDUCTION

Probably the most popular account of sexual seduction is found in the Book of Judges, chapters 14-16. The book introduces us to Samson, a Nazarene a man who was devoted to God. (1) Nazarenes never drank wine, (2) never went near a dead body (3) and never cut their hair.

Samson the strongest man of his generation never lived up to his promise as a Nazarene. Why? Samson had a weakness for women. He was unable to control his lust. When he saw an attractive woman, he wanted her. He first fell for a young woman he saw in a Philistine village just across the valley from his home. His parents tried to dissuade him, since her religion and culture were unacceptable, but he would not listen. Desire and lust was his only rule. The marriage ended in a matter of days and resulted in dozens of deaths. The famous Delilah was at least the third woman who dallied with Samson, according to the Book of Judges.

She, like his first love, was a Philistine living near his home. Where thousands of men had failed to overcome Samson, a Philistine woman who knew that somewhere and somehow all men are like little boys deep inside succeeded. Men always respond to praise because men were born to praise and worship God. A woman who simply knows what to say to a man is difficult to turn down and I believe Delilah was a very smooth talker. She knew how to get Samson's attention. Thanks to her, he was captured, blinded, and set to work pushing a grinding machine. His final triumph was ironically fitting: blind and bound, brought out like a freak for a shouting crowd's amusement, he destroyed himself while wrecking vengeance on the crowd.

At his death, as throughout his life, it was hard to say who suffered most from Samson's hot temper: the Philistines or Samson. When you think of what God meant Samson to be, his life appears particularly tragic. Israel desperately needed a strong, confident leader, for the Philistines were moving in as masters, and many

Israelites were willing to let them do so. God intended Samson for great things. Unfortunately Samson didn't live up to his promises as a Nazarene because he had a weakness - he was given to fits of lust and temper. Rule (3) was probably the only part of the Nazarene vow he kept unto God -it required little self-discipline to let hair grow.

Despite all of Samson's weaknesses, God used him and he is mentioned in the Holy Bible's *"Hall of Fame"* **(Hebrews 11:32)**, as a hero of faith together with Gideon, Barak and Jephtath, all from Judges. All though Samson had great physical strength, which came supernaturally from God's Spirit, as far as we can see; fruits of the Spirit like Love and Self-control seem lacking from his life.

2 Samuel chapters 11 -13, it mentions another man who like Samson was prone to lust. His name was David the King of Israel. His land Israel was now at peace and his beloved country was entering unprecedented prosperity after years of civil war, but he had let sin spread through him like cancer. One night David caught a glimpse of a woman's beautiful naked body and lusted after her and impulsively sent for her. The woman was called Bathsheba. The cover-up required murder - murder of her husband Uriah. Nobody could deny it was an ugly business: even David admitted it when Nathan confronted it. However, it was soon over. He repented and he married Bathsheba.

David never intended to fall into that temptation again, but the consequences of the sin were far from over. Unknown to David, cancer (sin) was growing in his own household. David's oldest son Amnon had an eye for women too. He tricked his half sister Tamar into his bedroom, and then raped her. Afterwards, filled with disgust, he threw her out. David was furious. But, maybe because he felt his own sin had robbed him of moral authority, he did nothing to punish his son. According to the law **(Leviticus 18:9, 29)**, Amnon deserved exile, but he went free. David apparently wanted the matter forgotten. It merely disappeared from view.

Absalom waited two full years to avenge his sister's rape. Then he murdered Amnon in cold blood. Again David was long on regret, short on punishment. He wept over Amnon's death but perhaps recognised his own responsibility for it.

The Holy Bible has a place of warning against adultery. It is found in the **Book of Proverbs chapters 5 and 6**, a book written by Solomon the son of King David.

(Please read this passage of Scripture for yourself).

WHOM SHOULD I MARRY THEN?

A good partner can make or break your life. In ancient times women were often viewed as men's property, good for bearing children and not much more. **The Book of Proverbs**, addressed to young men approaching the age of marriage, takes a different view. It holds up marriage as a crucial choice, to be made with great care. A good wife (or husband, we can assume) will make or break her partner's life. Her duties lay the foundation for her family's welfare **(14:1; 31:10-31)**. She shares with her husband the most significant task of teaching their children the way of wisdom **(1:8-9; 6:20)**. Therefore, her character matters far more than her physical beauty. Not that Proverbs ignores the physical side of love. It urges marriage partners to rejoice in their love, to be captivated by it (5:18-19). It warns young people against Sexual sin precisely because this wastes Sexuality on unsatisfying, unloving relationships. Sex ought to be saved therefore for the long-lasting, productive joy of marriage.

Proverbs on Sexual sin:

2:16-19; 5:1-23; 6:20-35; 7:6-27; 23:26-28.

Proverbs on Marriage:

5:15-19; 12:4; 14:1; 18:22; 19:13-14; 21:9, 19; 27:15-16; 31:10-31.

(Please study these Holy Scriptures for yourself and show yourself approved of God)

In the New Testament, and the **Book of 1 Corinthians chapter 7,** the Apostle Paul gives his personal opinions and discusses the thorny issue of singleness and marriage to the church. He carefully distinguishes what is his personal opinion and what is clear revelation from God. He explains in 29 why he reached these conclusions. In the same book, in **chapter 5,** Paul also speaks about avoiding Sexual immorality. And in the Book of **Colossians chapter 3, verses 5-6,** he comments on Holy Living. The call to purity, Paul speaks of is found in the **Book of 1 Thessalonians chapter 4, verses 1-8.**

The Lord Jesus Christ the founder of Christianity, gave a famous speech on the Sermon on the Mount, found in the **Book of Matthew chapter 5,** concerning Lust and Adultery, these words should be still applied to a world that lacks morality. To me personally and so many others world-wide, to the greatest question asked : **"What is LOVE?",** was answered by Jesus Christ, 2,000 years ago at a place called Golgotha - on Calvary Hill did the Son Of God, the Son of Man pay the ultimate sacrifice for the whole world's sin.

MARRIAGE

(Talking it over with your spouse)

I have learnt from my own marriage that *Communication* and *Listening* are vital and probably the most important two words for any married couple. In this chapter on the topic of Marriage, I have brought to the readers attention certain discussion points, that I trust will both instruct and inspire both men and women who are about to marry or who are already married, on what not to say or what not to do. My prayer is that your marriage will be a blessed one. That you and your spouse will always love and talk to each other; always forgiving one another regardless of who is right!

MARRIAGE

Marriage is about giving, not taking. When you marry a person, you marry everything they are and everything they have been. You inherit their strengths, their fears and their weaknesses. It's impossible to choose the parts you want and leave the ones you don't. Marriage – It's a package deal!

Marriage involves caring for each other ……..wanting to please your spouse. Your first ministry *is* to your own home ….. Your first vocation (calling) *is* to your spouse. Your priorities need to begin there, and then they can spread to your chosen career, your calling and other pursuits. Remember, God built the house, but we (married couples) have to do our own decorating!!

If you are reading this book, and you are experiencing marital problems, then I advise you my friend that you must go back to God, and He will give you the grace to minister to your spouse (and to the child within them). Be patient my friend! You may not see immediate change. It takes time for even a small cut to heal. It's a process. If you ask God, the author, developer and finisher of all marriages, He will give you the oil of compassion and the wine of His sweet agape love, to pour into your wounds. Don't settle for a Band-Aid or Elastoplast solution, only settle for God's total love restoration and peace in your marriage where there's turmoil.

Let Him through His unending, agape, unconditional love mend and heal your broken heart and turn-a-round everything from bad to good in your marriage. He is well able to do the impossible - for He is the same God yesterday, today and forever more!

Most couples begin their life together with very positive, definite ideas on how they want their marriage to work. Often these ideas are coloured by the images of wedded bliss presented in all the glossy adverts you see on the television, or read in the magazines — and it can be a shock to discover that life is not quite so straightforward. A lot of people find it hard to get the right balance between being their own person and being one half of a couple. If the relationship gives each person the time and space they need to do what interests them, fine. If not, there may be trouble ahead. Not so long ago women expected to give up work when they married so that they could stay at home and bring up children. Nowadays, many women are much more than this, which puts a strain on many marriages. Wives find themselves having to choose between their careers and starting a family — or trying to do both.

When both partners work, many husbands automatically assume that their career is more important. If the husband loses his job, leaving his wife as the family breadwinner, he may find it impossible to come to terms with how his life has changed.

Children of course change the lives of both partners forever. Once a couple have children they have to accept that they no longer have the freedom to do exactly what *they* want, when they want to. The woman may have to accept that she has to give up work, at least until the children start school. Having children is tiring too and partners find that they now have too little time simply to enjoy one another's company.

SINGLE PARENTING

Fourteen per cent of all families are one parent families in England, and the single parent is usually a woman. Single mothers are likely to lead much more stressful lives than women with partners to share the worries of child-raising. Between five and nine per cent of married women with children living at home go to their doctor with help with mental health problems, compared to 27 per cent of single mothers bringing up their families in cities or towns, and 13 per cent of single mothers living in country areas. There are many stressful problems facing single parents both women and men, and here is a list of them:

- Loneliness

- Poor housing

- For working parents – the cost of childminders and little time or energy to enjoy their children

- Part-time work is badly paid and reduces social security benefits

- Social security benefits are so low that the family may be forced into poverty

- Fathers may have to adjust to the idea of doing what is still seen as 'women's work'

Improvements in any of the above areas would simply relieve some of the stress in the lives of single parents.

DIVORCE

More and more couples whose marriage has not worked out are deciding to call it a day. Divorce is on the increase. Marriages which end in this way last for an average of 11 years when there are children and 7.5 years where there are not. Separation and divorce is the second most stressful life experience. The first is the death of a partner. Most people who get divorced wonder where they went wrong and whether they should have tried harder to make their marriage work. They find it difficult to admit that they have failed to keep the marriage alive and to deal with their feelings of anger, rejection, guilt, hurt, grief and emptiness. Coping with the stress of divorce can mean coming to terms with many things, for example loss. The loss of love and affection, loss of sexual relationship; perhaps loss of a dearly-loved home, and daily contact with the children can trigger stress related problems. Divorce is even more distressing when there are children involved. They are likely to feel hurt and rejected because *"Daddy's or Mummy's left us"* , and will be under pressure to *'be good'*.

In large families the oldest may have to take charge of the younger

ones while trying to support the parent who is left behind. The

situation is stressful for parents and children alike.

RECOGNISING THE SYMPTOMS IN MARRIAGE

Unless you are living by yourself on some remote desert island,

you know all too well the pain of broken relationships. Even the

very best of friendships can turn sour. All Marriages have their

'bad hair' days. Office workers can turn their office into a war-

zone. Churches argue and split over denominational differences or

personality conflicts. Close families explode because someone said

an unkind word. Neighbours argue amongst themselves concerning

parking space; barking dogs; and how high they are allowed to

have their fence. The problem is reaching epidemic proportions

and it is a greater threat to our well-being than influenza, breast

cancer, or heart disease. As with physical disorders, there are

certain tell-tale signs that normally point to the problem. Like

flashing blue lights, these symptoms warn that something is

seriously wrong. You can probably recognise the following symptoms from your own experiences.

Avoidance.

Long time friends suddenly avoid each other after an heated argument. Although they used to enjoy one another's company; now when they set their eyes on each other they keep their distance. They become **Irritable.** *"What did you say?" "Shut up, leave me alone!" "She makes me sick!" "Mind your own business!" "So what?", "I said no and I mean NO!" "I've had it with you!" "Get off my back, will you!"*

Do you recognise any of these fiery phrases? I'm sure you do. We've all heard them. And if you're honest with yourself right now, you will admit that you've said some of them.

Silence.

A common response to a wounded relationship is to apply the *"cold turkey"* strategy; silent treatment. We simply refuse to talk with the other person. It's a non-verbal signal that says, "I don't want to have anything to do with you anymore, so back off and leave me alone!" For some it is a way to insulate themselves from any other further damage or pain. For others, it is a way to get even. By refusing to talk, they hope to humiliate or make the other person suffer.

Recruiting allies.

It's rather unfortunate but some people respond to broken relationships like nations that have declared war on each other. They immediately enlist allies (so-called friends), by giving their view of the issue. And this one-sided account is the ammunition used in the battle. Such behaviour reveals insecurity and weakness. It exposes a person's lack of confidence to handle the problem adequately on their own.

Terrorism.

Like its counterpart in our world of bombings and hijackings, this form of personal aggression is subtle and comes without any warning. With methods that are indirect and underhanded, it often destroys the innocent along with the supposed enemy. There are angry looks and words, and even in some cases violent physical abuse. At times it may involve slanderous attacks, causing the destruction of someone's character or influence. If you see any or recognise these symptoms in your marriage or relationship's, then NOW is the time to resolve the problem before it gets any worse!

DON'T MAKE IT ANY WORSE.

Poison Ivy can make life miserable. The rash it causes itself is hard to take but, the urge to itch or scratch is sheer torture. To give in to the overwhelming temptation to rub or scratch, though, only makes the problem far worse. The poison spreads, and the agony is compounded. The right solution to the predicament is to apply some healing cream and to keep from doing what itchy skin cries out for you to do. Likewise, broken relationships can make life miserable too. But, like dealing with poison ivy, our natural response may only make matters worse. Many times our attempts to fix the solutions just don't work. To avoid making those kinds of mistakes, let us now look at some tactics that we can apply that are ineffective or self-defeating in marriages.

Ignoring the problem.

The largest bird in the world today, the Ostrich, has the undeserved reputation of responding to imminent danger by sticking its head in the sand. That might seem foolish. Yet, many people unfortunately respond just like an Ostrich in a similar way in broken relationships, and married life. Ignoring a problem allows it to spread like a cancer, eating away at the relationship.

Attack the person.

We may make the fatal mistake of attacking the person instead of the issue. Often the original cause of the conflict is forgotten. Name-calling or faultfinding takes over and builds a wall that hides the real issue.

Manipulate.

Sometimes we are more interested in getting things to work out for our own personal interests. We may feel that we have all the right answers and will work to get others to see things our way. This in reality is a subtle form of pride and selfishness.

Involving the wrong people.

We may even mistakenly involve those individuals who are more interested in spreading gossip than in restoring relationships.

Talking too much.

Are we good listeners? Do we lend an ear and try to understand our partner's our spouses our loved ones? It's not enough just to be on the talking end of an issue.

Neglect timing and tact.

We may do and say the right things but not get the results we expected. If our efforts lack caution, proper timing and loving tact, we will only unfortunately compound the problem.

Covering it up.

"Oh, just forget it." "Let's put it all behind us, and let's start all over again." These and other similar statements are good if they express genuine reconciliation. But they are inadequate if they are nothing more than plasters on a broken arm. Wounds inflicted in the heart need more than superficial words.

Discarding it.

Sometimes, relationships are treated like disposable goods. If something goes wrong, it seems more trouble than it's worth to patch things up. Some may even suggest that the best solution is to end the association completely. Yes, broken relationships can be made worse instead of better if we handle them the wrong way. The necessary repair work can be accomplished in your marital home, when we are willing to follow the pattern of the author, and finisher of all Marriages – who is God Almighty!!

DISCUSSION RULES

- Discussions should be held in order to *reach a solution*, not to gain a victory!

- *Discuss one thing at time* and the basic outline of a discussion should be: State your problem, suggest an alternative, and reach a solution!

- *You cannot refuse a discussion*. If something is important to one member of the marriage, it is worth discussing!

- State your problem in the form of a *request*, not a demand. If the discussion is a question of *fact*, then it is your duty to get the facts!

- If the discussion is a *matter of opinion*, you must recognise it as such and realise that a *compromise is the only solution*

- *Don't try to mind-read.* It's impossible, so ask instead, and *don't try to play the psychologist!*

- Don't try to tell others what they are thinking or why they are doing something. This covers our most famous rule: *don't assume!*

- *Don't play the archaeologist!* Don't dig things out of the past; discuss your present problems with one another.

- *Don't make speeches!* State your problem, and then let the other person answer.

- If your partner states a point, you *must* respond to it before you can make a new one!

Answer questions directly!

- *No emotional blackmail.* "If you really loved me, you

would!"

- You can state your problems about observations of *behaviour, not judgements on states of being!*

Never interrupt!

Go back to the 1st discussion rule listed, **and never forget it!!**

** REMEMBER **

ALL DISCUSSIONS SHOULD ALWAYS BE HELD

IN ORDER TO REACH A SOLUTION,

NOT TO GAIN A VICTORY!!

Dear reader, now it's study time for you – so please read, meditate and pray upon the scripture references listed on the following next page, found in the Holy Bible – God's Word, and believe for your marriage to grow even stronger in love; intimacy; peace; joy; happiness; harmony always and, to remain a blessed one, in Jesus' magnificent name. The Bible says we are to spend time studying the Word of God, then we will be blessed and have His divine approval. My friend, there is salvation; abundant life; blessings; healing; deliverance in God's Word, and it can heal us everywhere we hurt!

Remember, also, *it is* very good to talk – you must talk and not shout at one another!

USE THESE SCRIPTURES

Ephesians 4: 2-3

1 Corinthians 14: 40

Romans 12: 10

Proverbs 20: 3

John 8: 32

Philippians 2: 1-4

1 Corinthians 2: 11

1 Thessalonians 3: 3-14

James 1: 19

Proverbs 15: 23

James 3: 10

1 Peter 3: 10

Romans 14: 13

Galatians 6: 1

Matthew 7: 1

Hebrews 13:4

LOVE *is SACRIFICE*

I have a question to ask you right now: **"How many people do you know who love you so much that they would give their life for you?"** I don't know anyone except Jesus Christ of Nazareth, who not only showed His unconditional agape Love for me personally, but He showed it for the whole world, regardless of age, or colour, or culture when he hung on the Cross for all to see and experience what true Love is. This portion of Scripture found in the Book of John chapter 3, verse 16 in the New Testament, sums up the whole of the "Gospel" of the Lord Jesus Christ in a nutshell:

"For God so loved the world that He gave His one and only Son (Jesus), that whosoever believes in Him shall not perish but have everlasting life."

Throughout the Holy Bible we are shown that God wants a very close, personal, loving relationship with His children and intimacy with us as He had with Jesus. A father or mother will bend down to a little child, pick him up and hold him close. The child will be comforted when anxious, helped when troubled, encouraged when despondent, guided when unsure and have every need provided.

Our God is doing that to us every single day. His heart is open to us, His hand outstretched, in love, and He looks for that love to be returned by us to Him.

Dear reader, my prayer is that you too will experience God's Love, through His Son Jesus. God gave His only Son Jesus, to die for you personally. He shed His precious blood for you personally on the Cross, and He resurrected on the Third Day, so that you would have everlasting life personally, with Him in Heaven as He promised in the Holy Bible.

Jesus Christ said in the Book of John chapter 14 and verse 6, *"I am the Way, the Truth, and the Life. No-one comes to the Father (God) except through Me."* And in the same book of John, chapter 3, verse 3, Jesus also said that *"no-one can see the kingdom of God unless he is born again."* Verse 7, Jesus spoke direct and truthful by saying, *"You must be born again."*

- (1 Peter 3: 18) says: *"For Christ died for sins once and for all, the righteous for the unrighteous to bring you to God."*

- (Acts 4:12) says: **"Salvation is found in no-one else, for there is no other name under heaven given to men by which we must be saved."**

- (Romans 6:23) says: **"For the wages of sin is death, but the, but the gift of God is eternal life in Christ Jesus our Lord."**

(In the same Book of Romans chapter 10, verse 9 and verse 10), it says: ***"That if you confess with your mouth, 'Jesus is Lord', and believe in your heart that God raised Him from the dead, you will be saved. For it is with your heart that you believe and are justified*** *(just-as-if -you've-never-sinned),* ***and it is with your mouth that you confess and are saved."*** (*Italics mine*).

My friend, unless you have peace with God, your life will always be in pieces! God wants a personal relationship with you. He wants to better your individual life, spiritually, mentally, emotionally, physically and financially. He promised us through His Son Jesus, in the **(Book of John 10:10)**, a more abundant life. In the **(Book of Matthew chapter 28:20),** Jesus promised us all, that He would be with us always, to the very end of age.

Stop putting your trust in men or women, who have failed you, and let you down. Start putting your trust in someone who has never ever let any person down - Jesus Christ!

All you have to do is believe in Him, accept Him as your Lord and personal Saviour, then you will obtain everlasting life that He promised us and also inherit all the blessings of God, He also promised unto all His children (believers), found in the Holy Bible. God loves *you!* In any language there are no more wonderful words. God showed us that unique unconditional love by sending His Son Jesus Christ, into the world as a man to suffer and die on the Cross in our place and rise again to conquer sin and death. Such great love requires a personal response.

Today, my friend if you would like to surrender your life right now to Jesus Christ, and to have a personal everyday relationship with Him, and to make Him Lord over every situation of your life, then please repeat this sinner's prayer from your heart aloud. For Jesus promised everyone: ***"Believe in the name of the Lord Jesus, and you will be saved - you and your household."***

(Acts 16:31)

PRAYER FOR YOURSELF

"Lord, thank you for sending Your Son Jesus to die for me on the Cross. I am turning away from my sin and rebellion today to receive Jesus Christ into my heart, and into my life right now as my personal Saviour and Lord and my very best friend, in His name I pray." - AMEN.

Dear friend, if you prayed this above prayer I welcome you to the family of God (the Body of Christ). I pray that you will find now find a born again Christian church that believes in the Holy Bible and the gifts of the Holy Spirit near where you live to fellowship with other fellow Christians. I pray that you will purchase a Holy Bible if you don't already have one, and read it everyday. And, lastly as a Christian you must pray to God everyday!

SEX

before Marriage.
What's the harm then?

Unique

WRITING PUBLICATIONS

Unique Writing Publications (UK)

Books written by Daniele Luciano Moskal

Jesus His-story, UNEXPLAINABLE yet UNDENIABLE

Prayers of the Old Testament

Many are Called but Few are Chosen

Fragile Handle with Care

Little Hedge King

I must 'Be-About' My Father's Business

Your Life is a Story

If you would like to contact **Evangelist Daniele Luciano Moskal** concerning any of his books or his ministries, you can do so by sending him an email at this address:
penofareadywriter@hotmail.co.uk

www.ingramcontent.com/pod-product-compliance
Lightning Source LLC
Chambersburg PA
CBHW031333040426
42443CB00005B/318